WHY IRAN'S 2021 ELECTION IS DIFFERENT

Explosive Society, Impending Boycott, Unprecedented Purge

NATIONAL COUNCIL OF RESISTANCE OF IRAN
U.S. REPRESENTATIVE OFFICE

Why Iran's 2021 Election Is Different;
Explosive Society, Impending Boycott, Unprecedented Purge

Copyright © National Council of Resistance of Iran – U.S. Representative Office, 2021.

All rights reserved. No part of this monograph may be used or reproduced in any manner whatsoever without written permission except in the case of brief quotations embodied in articles or reviews.

First published in 2021 by
National Council of Resistance of Iran - U.S. Representative Office (NCRI-US),
1747 Pennsylvania Ave., NW, Suite 1125, Washington, DC 20006

ISBN-10 (paperback): 1-944942-42-4
ISBN-13 (paperback): 978-1-944942-42-7

ISBN-10 (e-book): 1-944942-43-2
ISBN-13 (e-book): 978-1-944942-43-4

Library of Congress Control Number: 2021911251
Library of Congress Cataloging-in-Publication Data

National Council of Resistance of Iran - U.S. Representative Office.
Why Iran's 2021 Election Is Different

1. Iran. 2. Elections. 3. Corruption. 4. Human Rights. 5. Economy.

First Edition: May 2021

Printed in the United States of America

These materials are being distributed by the National Council of Resistance of Iran-U.S. Representative Office. Additional information is on file with the Department of Justice, Washington, D.C.

Table of Contents

Introduction. 5

Summary 7

Elections under the Velayat-e Faqih Theocracy 11
    Why the Velayat-e Faqih Needs a President 12
    Only Candidates Loyal to the Supreme Leader Can Run 13
    President's Powers Are Limited 14

Why the 2021 Election Is Different 15
    Unprecedented Purge. 16
    Game-Changing Uprisings Since 2017 Election. 17
    Corruption and Unjust Distribution of Wealth 18
    All-out Boycott Feared for Months 19
    Criminally Incompetent Handling of COVID-19 Pandemic 20
    Furious Factional Infighting 21
    Rivals Vie for Power 22
    Election Process Excludes Any Qualified Contender 23
    A Weak, Vulnerable Regime 24

Successive Uprisings Since 2017, the Game Changer 25

**The Economy & Corruption Weigh Heavily
on Iran's Elections.** 31
    How Did the Economy Reach This Point? 32
    "Misery Index" Soaring 34
    60 Million Living Below the Poverty Line 35
    Will a Return to the JCPOA Cure the Economy? 36

- Systemic Corruption 37
- Economic Issues, Corruption Sparked Recent Uprisings 37
- Empty Tables, Public Outrage, An Electoral Boycott 39

Historic Boycott Expected 41
- Widespread Electoral Apathy 43
- Call for a Boycott by Maryam Rajavi 45
- The Regime's Worst Nightmare 49

The Candidates 53
- Ebrahim Raisi 54
- Saeed Jalili 57
- Mohsen Rezaee 58
- Mohsen Mehralizadeh 59
- Alireza Zakani 60
- Abdolnaser Hemmati 61
- Amir-Hossein Ghazizadeh Hashemi 62

The Selection Process 63
- The Five Qualifications 64
- Added Criteria to Restrict Registration 65
- Proportion of rejected candidates in 13 presidential elections 66
- Supreme Leader's 4 Filters for a President 67

What's Ahead? 71

List of publications 73

About NCRI-US 79

Introduction

Elections in Iran have never been about expressing the popular choice in a democratic, fair and transparent process. They are, rather, a selection process by the *Velayat-e Faqih* who is himself unelected. The Iran regime's Supreme Leader, Ali Khamenei, controls the Guardian Council, an unelected vetting body charged with filtering candidates. As such, the election outcome is not decided by the people, but by the regime's internal balance of power.

While every election since 1979 has been rigged, they have served to give an appearance of democracy and republicanism to the ruling theocracy. The 2021 election is, however, vastly different, because Iran in 2021 is on the threshold of a fundamental transformation.

Khamenei finds his regime increasingly weak and vulnerable following a series of uprisings since 2017, endemic corruption, and a bankrupt economy. The explosive state of Iranian society was reflected in the crushing blow of the 2020 parliamentary election boycott, and in the growing prowess of the nationwide organized opposition. All of these crises are aggravated by ferocious factional infighting. Faced with these realities, Khamenei has opted to close ranks and consolidate power in the hands of those absolutely loyal to him to prevent the seismic shift he knows is coming.

In a move driven by the Supreme Leader, the Guardian Council has disqualified several longtime establishment figures, most significantly Ali Larijani, the former speaker of the regime's parliament for 12 years. A former IRGC brigadier general and Secretary of the Supreme National Security Council, Larijani has been a senior advisor to Khamenei and a member of his inner circle.

Khamenei has now dispensed with the no-longer beneficial "moderate-hardliner" farce in favor of securing the presidency of his selected candidate, Judiciary Chief Ebrahim Raisi, notorious for his key role, as Deputy Prosecutor of Tehran and a member of the "death committee," in the executions of as many as 30,000 political prisoners, primarily activists of the People's Mojahedin Organization of Iran (MEK), in 1988. Raisi began his rise in the regime's hierarchy by ordering hundreds of other executions in the early 1980s.

By sacking his inner circle in favor of Raisi, his most loyal ally, Khamenei will rely heavily on Raisi as well as the IRGC to counter the popular discontent, as he will rely on the Qods Force to expand his proxies in Syria, Lebanon and Iraq. The more isolated he finds himself at home, the more he needs to count on such repressive institutions.

This election marks an end to the games and masquerades. It is now evident that the true fight is between the people and the organized opposition seeking freedom and democracy on the one side, and the entirety of the regime headed by Khamenei and Raisi and powered by the IRGC on the other.

The electoral purge is, however, only a stopgap, which will likely backfire, given the fragile state of the regime. Khamenei has alienated a significant segment of the establishment and further narrowed the theocracy's power base. The tide has shifted in favor of the people, who are expected to respond to the Supreme Leader with a massive boycott, the flip side of their desire to end the rule of the ayatollahs and establish a free and democratic republic.

The international community should realize that any negotiations are in fact with Supreme Leader Ali Khamenei and his mass murderer Raisi. They would do better to reach out to the people of Iran as a true and lasting partner.

Summary

The Iranian regime's 13th presidential election will be held on June 18, 2021. Registration of candidates ended on May 15; a total of 592 individuals registered. The un-elected Guardian Council, a vetting body made up of six clerics appointed by the Supreme Leader and six jurists selected by the Supreme Leader appointee, the head of Judiciary, and approved by him, reviews their qualifications and announces the final list of candidates within ten days. On May 25, the Guardian Council decision was released for the 2021 election sham, only 7 were approved from among 592 who registered. Campaigning follows until June 17, 2021.

Unprecedented Purge: In a move driven by the Supreme Leader, the Guardian Council has disqualified several longtime establishment figures, most significantly Ali Larijani, the former speaker of the regime's parliament for 12 years. A former IRGC brigadier general and Secretary of the Supreme National Security Council, Larijani has been a senior advisor to Khamenei and a member of his inner circle. Khamenei has now dispensed with the no-longer beneficial "moderate-hardliner" farce in favor of securing the presidency of his selected candidate, Judiciary Chief Ebrahim Raisi.

Presidential Elections under the *Velayat-e Faqih* Theocracy: Under the theocratic regime's Constitution, the presidency has little impact on Iran's domestic or foreign policy since both are set by the regime's Supreme Leader, Ali Khamenei. The electoral process is stage-managed and tightly controlled to produce the desired results. Ballot numbers are regularly inflated several fold to imply popular participation. The presidency and the electoral process are strictures forced upon Khomeini's original concept of the absolute rule of the theocratic leader by domestic political pressure deriving from the Iranian people's century-long movement for freedom.

The 2021 Election is Different: Since 1979, every election in Iran has been rigged and engineered, and has served only to give an appearance of democracy and republicanism to a corrupt, brutal theocracy. All elections have also widened the schism among the regime's power-hungry factions. The upcoming election will be no different. The 13th presidential election, however, is vastly different from those before it, primarily because it is taking place when the theocratic regime is at its most precarious state since 1979, and its prospects of survival are openly questioned by regime insiders and challenged by a restive, freedom-seeking nation.

Uprisings Since the 2017 Election: This year's election is heavily impacted by a series of major social upheavals, including the 2017, 2018, and 2019 uprisings, whose main slogan was: "Hardliners, reformers, the game is now over," and "Death to the dictator," shaking the foundations of the regime in its entirety. The images of these martyrs and scenes of the many murdered in cold blood will never leave the Iranian people's psyche. These uprisings showed that the Iranian people are now focused on overthrowing the regime, and no longer pin any hope on elections as a conduit for substantive change.

Economic Crisis and Systemic Corruption: Iran's regime has been plagued by institutionalized financial corruption since its inception. The regime's economic incompetence, systemic corruption, and outright plunder of the country's wealth have pushed more people below the poverty line. The consequent financial and social misery and unprecedented economic divide between ordinary citizens and the ruling elite are motivating Iranians to boycott the upcoming presidential election. They see the corrupt ruling theocracy as their true enemy and the first and foremost cause of the economic crises. One of the most dominant slogans in the recent uprisings has been, "Our enemy is right here; they lie when they say it is America."

All-out Boycott: The regime's studies of public attitudes predict and express concern over a lower turnout worse that the February 2020 parliamentary elections. The expected nationwide boycott is not a passive response to the ruling theocracy. It is indeed the flipside of the nationwide desire for regime change. A wide range of social sectors, from small investors in the stock market to pensioners, nurses, farmers, and workers, have joined the call for a massive boycott.

Iranian Resistance's Call for Boycott: Following a call by the Iranian Resistance's President-elect, Maryam Rajavi, the network of the People's Mojahedin Organization of Iran (PMOI/MEK) in Iran has been leading a nationwide campaign to boycott Iran's sham presidential election. In various cities, graffiti by Resistance Units declares: "No to the sham elections," "My vote is for regime change," "Boycotting the election sham is a patriotic duty," "No to the mullahs' rule, no to religious tyranny, yes to a democratic republic," and "Down with Khamenei."

Criminally Incompetent Handling of COVID-19 Pandemic: Khamenei's heartless COVID-19 policy decisions, as well as the outright lies and false promises about vaccine availability of the regime's president, Hassan Rouhani, have enraged the nation. On the anniversary of the Iran-Iraq war last year, Khamenei asserted that the pandemic has been a "blessing" for his regime. He has sought to exploit the pandemic. Khamenei's gamble, however, has failed. Instead, it has further enraged a restive population already ravaged by poverty and corruption and a long list of economic and social miseries and natural disasters.

Furious Factional Infighting: Never in the past four decades have the internal rivalries within the ruling system been this ferocious. Following the series of uprisings, the suffocating pressure of international sanctions, and particularly the crushing blow of the boycott of the 2020 parliamentary elections, Khamenei finds himself increasingly weak and vulnerable in the regime's internal balance of power. To compensate, he instructed the Guardian Council to approve candidates who, while representing their individual leanings, must be totally loyal to him. These developments portend a presidential election characterized by the same trend of a Khamenei push to solidify in the face of popular discontent and international isolation.

A Weak, Vulnerable Regime: The November 2019 uprising in particular was a rude awakening, during which the regime saw that despite its multi-layered, multi-faceted security forces, it was in fact very vulnerable. The events demonstrated to the world that the Tehran regime can be overthrown. The situation of Iran's ruling elite has been further aggravated by ferocious factional infighting, in turn worsened by the protests. Adding to that, international sanctions and major shifts in regional alignments due in large part to threats posed by Tehran to the security and stability of the region, have substantially weakened the entire ruling system.

Seismic Shift Is Coming: Iranian society is simmering with deeply rooted rage. Iran is a powder keg, where anything, even a sudden rise in the price of fuel or eggs, could trigger a nationwide revolt. Khamenei and his regime are trying in vain to prevent the seismic shift they know is coming. This election will only speed up the disintegration of the regime which would lead to the overthrow of clerical regime.

Elections under the Velayat-e Faqih Theocracy

Elections in Iran are a farce. Since Khamenei succeeded Khomeini in 1989 as a much weaker Supreme Leader, he has faced skeptical regime loyalists split into power-sharing factions. The factions vie for turns at the presidency to profit their beneficiaries. The farcical nature of the elections is highlighted by the several-fold multiplication of ballot numbers in election headquarters where both factions are present, to imply popular participation in the vote. In the last election cycle, nearly five million fraudulent votes were stuffed into ballot boxes in some precincts. The election headquarters announced a ludicrous four-fold 73% participation rate.

This corrupt, restricted electoral process is further controlled in numerous ways, the exclusionary list of candidates being only the first step. The process of electoral "engineering" involves each faction trying to outmaneuver the other by various machinations, through vote-buying, intimidation, and outright ballot- box stuffing.

Why the Velayat-e Faqih Needs a President

The Supreme Leader, as the vicegerent of God on earth answering only to the Almighty, has total power and no accountability, whereas the president, though seemingly elected by popular vote, must be confirmed by the Supreme Leader.

The presidency and the electoral process are strictures forced upon Khomeini's original concept of the absolute rule of the theocratic leader by domestic political pressure deriving from the Iranian people's century-long movement for freedom. As such, the electoral process under this regime is stage-managed and tightly controlled to produce results that both factions can accept, while not violating the absolute authority of the

Supreme Leader, which underpins the system and is a red line. In short, elections in Iran are a travesty of the electoral process.

While the office of the presidency is meant to provide a pretense of democratic literacy for the ruling theocracy, as an institution it introduces an unintended instability in the rule of the Supreme Leader, and sooner or later stands in contrast to his absolute rule. Many of the previous presidents were ostracized after completing their terms.

Only Candidates Loyal to the Supreme Leader Can Run

Article 115 of the regime's Constitution and Article 35 of the election law set the threshold for presidential candidates to Muslim males, faithful to the "Islamic Republic," and with practical belief and commitment to the principle of the *Velayat-e-Faqih* (absolute clerical rule). The unelected and handpicked Guardian Council added exclusions in 2021 in a tactical adjustment to further disqualify and curtail potentially troublesome candidates from the self-proclaimed "Reformist" camp in the upcoming elections.

The Guardian Council routinely disqualifies numerous candidates, especially women, based on the regime's exclusionary electoral process and Khamenei's assent. Only loyalist males who have demonstrated their absolute allegiance to the Supreme Leader, as the sole indisputable source of power, are permitted to run.

In 2013 and 2017, the Council disqualified two-term presidents Akbar Hashemi Rafsanjani and Mahmoud Ahmadinejad, based on their falling out with Khamenei, even though they had previously been deemed qualified to run and serve as President.

President's Powers Are Limited

The presidency is essentially regarded as ineffectual and has little impact on Iran's domestic or especially foreign policy. Former President Mohammad Khatami famously described his role as that of a mere functionary. All policy is set by the Supreme Leader through various agencies controlled by his office, and the executive branch is challenged by parallel Islamic Republic Guard Corps (IRGC) controlled power centers. Yet the presidency affords the winner a commanding role in state organizations and agencies that sit atop a corrupt oligarchy controlling Iran's national wealth, including control of the oil, gas, and petrochemical industry that fuels Iran's corrupt rentier regime.

The election results tend to reflect the balance of power among factions. In 2005, Supreme Leader Ali Khamenei decided to consolidate his rule by securing Mahmoud Ahmadinejad's election through electoral engineering. In 2009, Ahmadinejad won via the same process despite widespread public outcry.

Khamenei failed to push through his own choice in the 2013 and 2017 elections, however, and Hassan Rouhani became president. The Principlists loyal to Khamenei tend to rely on voter intimidation and overt fraud, whereas the opposing faction rely on hollow promises to improve the lives of the citizens. Both factions vie for an increasingly paltry segment of the electorate, who are openly challenging the regime's authority in the streets with chants of, "We won't vote anymore; we've heard too many lies."

Why the 2021 Election Is Different

Since 1979, every election in Iran has been rigged and engineered, and has served only to give an appearance of democracy and republicanism to a corrupt, brutal theocracy. Whatever any election's outcome, the Supreme Leader, as the vicegerent of God on earth answering only to the Almighty, retains total power and no accountability. All elections have also widened the schism among the regime's power-hungry factions. The upcoming election will be no different.

The 13th presidential election, however, is vastly different than those before it, primarily because it is taking place when the theocratic regime is at its most precarious state since 1979, and its prospects of survival are openly questioned by regime insiders and challenged by a restive, freedom-seeking nation. There are several main reasons why:

Unprecedented Purge

Khamenei finds his regime increasingly weak and vulnerable following a series of uprisings since 2017, endemic corruption, and a bankrupt economy. The explosive state of Iranian society was reflected in the crushing blow of the 2020 parliamentary election boycott, and in the growing prowess of the nationwide organized opposition. All of these crises are aggravated by ferocious factional infighting. Faced with these realities, Khamenei has opted to close ranks and consolidate power in the hands of those absolutely loyal to him to prevent the seismic shift he knows is coming.

In a move driven by the Supreme Leader, the Guardian Council has disqualified several longtime establishment figures, most significantly Ali Larijani, the former speaker of the regime's parliament for 12 years. A former IRGC brigadier general and Secretary of the Supreme National

Security Council, Larijani has been a senior advisor to Khamenei and a member of his inner circle. Khamenei has now dispensed with the no-longer beneficial "moderate-hardliner" farce in favor of securing the presidency of his selected candidate, Judiciary Chief Ebrahim Raisi.

The electoral purge is, however, only a stopgap, which will likely backfire, given the fragile state of the regime. Khamenei has alienated a significant segment of the establishment and further narrowed the theocracy's power base.

Game-Changing Uprisings Since 2017 Election

The uprisings in December 2017, January 2018, November 2019, and January 2020 have changed the conditions for both factions who fear, among other things, the eruption of another round of protests. During the December 2017 — January 2018 uprising, only six months after the June 2017 elections, the Iranian people emphatically rejected both factions and sought the regime's ouster, as expressed in slogans prevalent throughout the protests: "Hardliner, reformer, the game is now over," "Down with Khamenei, down with Rouhani," and "Death to the dictator."

The November 2019 uprising encompassed nearly 200 cities and towns. The Islamic Revolutionary Guard Corps opened fire on protesters almost immediately and killed approximately 1,500 people over the course of about two weeks. The images of these martyrs and scenes of the many murdered in cold blood will never leave the Iranian people's psyche. At a minimum, it will fuel their rejection of the regime and its elections.

These uprisings showed that the Iranian people are now focused on overthrowing the regime, and no longer pin any hope on elections as a conduit for substantive change. The people consider the regime and all its factions as illegitimate. In fact, the anti-regime reverberations of the November uprising as well as the January 2020 shooting down of a Ukrainian airliner with 176 passengers, were major factors in the lowest ever voter turnout in the 2020 parliamentary elections. The writing is on the wall: "My vote is for regime change."

Corruption and Unjust Distribution of Wealth

Iran's regime has been plagued by institutionalized financial corruption since its inception. According to Transparency International, Iran ranks 149 among 180 countries on the corruption perceptions index. The regime's economic incompetence, systemic corruption, and outright plunder of the country's wealth have pushed more people below the poverty line. The consequent financial and social misery and unprecedented economic divide between ordinary citizens and the ruling elite are motivating Iranians to boycott the upcoming presidential election.

Over 50% of Iranians now have access to smartphones and a multitude of social media platforms. They see in real time that as vital items such as meat, dairy products, poultry, and eggs disappear from their tables, the tables of the ruling elite and their families become more colorful and richer by the day.

They see the corrupt ruling theocracy as their true enemy and the first and foremost cause of the economic crises. One of the most dominant slogans in the recent uprisings has been, "Our enemy is right here; they lie when they say it is America." According to the regime's official statistics, more than 60 million of Iran's population of 80 million live below the poverty line. Today, the poverty line sits on top of the middle class. The citizens know well that, even if the regime manages to sell oil and natural resources in 2021, it still will not have a serious impact on their lives. They have firsthand experience: their living standard in fact decreased after the 2015 JCPOA, and much of the financial boom the regime enjoyed went into the coffers of the ruling elite and their proxy groups.

There are many indications from inside the country that the economically deprived, politically oppressed and marginalized segments of society will not only boycott the election farce, but are also focused on unleashing their rage on the regime.

All-out Boycott Feared for Months

The regime's studies of public attitudes predict and express concern over a lower turnout for the presidential election than the February 2020 parliamentary election farce. The Interior Ministry publicly put the February 2020 election turnout at 42% nationwide, and about 20% for Tehran. However, an internal Ministry report admitted the turnout was 20% nationwide and 9% in Tehran.

There is a consensus among all factions that a low turnout would deal an existential blow to the regime in so fragile a state. On May 11, Supreme Leader Ali Khamenei warned, "Primarily, a large popular turnout is important since [a low turnout] could turn into a security problem."

The expected nationwide boycott is not a passive response to the ruling theocracy. It is indeed the flipside of the nationwide desire for regime change. On May 16, Mohammad Ali Abtahi, Chief of Staff of former President Mohammad Khatami, acknowledged, "This time the main challenger in the election is neither a Reformist nor a Principlist; it is low voter turnout."

A wide range of social sectors, from small investors in the stock market to pensioners, nurses, farmers, and workers, have joined the call for a massive boycott. Earlier in May, many families of the martyrs of the November 2019 uprising bravely called for an election boycott with chants of "Our vote is regime change" and "Overthrow this regime."

Following a call by the Iranian Resistance's President-elect, Maryam Rajavi, the MEK network in Iran has been leading a nationwide campaign to boycott Iran's sham presidential election. In various cities, graffiti by Resistance Units declares: "No to the sham elections," "My vote is for regime change," "Boycotting the election sham is a patriotic duty," "No to the mullahs' rule, no to religious tyranny, yes to a democratic republic," and "Down with Khamenei."

Criminally Incompetent Handling of COVID-19 Pandemic

Khamenei's heartless COVID-19 policy decisions, among them banning internationally approved vaccines manufactured by the United States, United Kingdom, and France, as well as Rouhani's outright lies and false promises about vaccine availability, have enraged the nation. As of May 25, 2021, nearly 300,000 Iranians have lost their lives due to COVID-19, according to the most reliable information from inside Iran.

Back in April 2020, Khamenei described the COVID-19 pandemic as a test and a blessing, similar to his predecessor, Khomeini, who had labeled another national catastrophe, the Iran-Iraq War, as a "blessing."

The regime's Supreme Leader made the same ominous assertion again in September 2020 during his speech on the anniversary of the Iran-Iraq war, saying the pandemic has been a "blessing" for his regime.

Indeed, Khamenei has sought to exploit the pandemic to defuse the pre-COVID19 anti-regime momentum and shield his regime against future uprisings. His wicked game of numbers, under-reporting the COVID-19 fatalities by a factor of 4 or 5, must also be seen in this context.

Khamenei's gamble, however, has failed. Instead, it has further enraged a restive population already ravaged by poverty and corruption and a long list of economic and social miseries and natural disasters. The regime's cruel indifference to the lives of ordinary Iranians, tragically an all too familiar strategy, will only aggravate the intolerance of the ruling elite, hastening the inevitable regime change. The next uprising is coming and will be even more fierce due partly to the regime's mismanagement and exploitation of the COVID-19 pandemic. In the short term, however, it is another reason why a majority of Iranians are expected to boycott the election farce.

Furious Factional Infighting

Never in the past four decades have the internal rivalries within the ruling system been this ferocious. A kleptocracy will inherently be divided into competing political and economic tendencies, constantly at war with each other over a bigger share of the plunder of Iran's national wealth. Only when the survival of the system is at risk will they join hands to preserve it.

The infamous audio tape of Foreign Minister Javad Zarif talking about master terrorist Qassem Soleimani, leaked in April, fueled the already explosive infighting, to the point that Khamenei had to intervene and admonish Zarif for his utterance. That was the end of any chance for Zarif, hyped by some as the best hope of the "moderate/reformist" camp, to register as a candidate.

Following the series of uprisings, the suffocating pressure of international sanctions, and particularly the crushing blow of the boycott of the 2020 parliamentary elections, Khamenei finds himself increasingly weak and vulnerable in the regime's internal balance of power. To compensate, he has instructed the Guardian Council to approve candidates who, while representing their individual leanings, must be totally loyal to him. Khamenei's March 21 speech confirms that he has decided to retrench and consolidate his regime. In May 2020, he announced his desire for a "young *Hezbollahi* government."

These developments portend a presidential election characterized by the same trend of a Khamenei push to solidify in the face of popular discontent and international isolation. This was also the trend in the parliamentary elections in February 2020, when the Guardian Council disqualified most of the rival camp's candidates.

Rivals Vie for Power

The *Velayat-e-Faqih* regime consists of various mafia-like blocs grouped into two main factions, known as "Principlists" (*Osulgara:*) and "Reformists" (*Eslah Talab*). Although there are various tendencies within each, they may be summarized thus:

    A. The Principlists (pro-Khamenei faction) currently comprise four political blocs: The Unity Council, the Conservative Alliance, the Perseverance Front, and Ahmadinejad's faction. These factions, loosely coalesced around Khamenei, suffer from deep schisms, especially since the January 2018 and November 2019 uprisings. Each has invoked the criteria set by Khamenei to put forward its own candidate. None seems to be willing to withdraw in favor of the others.

B. The so-called Reformist faction, originally known as "Followers of the Imam's Line" (in reference to the regime's founder, Khomeini), played a key role in the U.S. embassy occupation, and in establishing and running the security services, the prisons, and launching the internal repression and external terrorism. After Khamenei became the Supreme Leader in 1989, this camp conveniently proclaimed itself to be "reformist." This faction faces two problems in the upcoming presidential election: 1) disqualification of its primary candidates by the Guardian Council, and 2) a nationwide election boycott, which would threaten its ability to impact the regime's internal balance of power.

Election Process Excludes Any Qualified Contender

The regime's Constitution and the election law set the threshold for presidential candidates to Muslim males, faithful to the "Islamic Republic," and with practical belief and commitment to the principle of the *Velayat-e-Faqih* (absolute clerical rule). The Guardian Council routinely disqualifies numerous candidates, especially women, based on the regime's exclusionary electoral process and Khamenei's assent. Only loyalist males who have demonstrated their absolute allegiance to the Supreme Leader, as the sole indisputable source of power, are permitted to run.

The Iranian people have emphatically declared during several nationwide uprisings and ongoing protests of varying sizes and locations, that they have no illusions that this rigged, restricted and corrupt electoral process will produce reform or gradual change from within the regime. They know the rival factions vie for turns at assuming the presidency only to profit their beneficiaries.

A Weak, Vulnerable Regime

The series of uprisings since 2017 dealt a major shock to the theocratic regime's foundations. The November 2019 uprising in particular was a rude awakening, during which the regime saw that despite its multi-layered, multi-faceted security forces, it was in fact very vulnerable. The events demonstrated to the world that the Tehran regime can be overthrown.

Unrest has continued, with daily protests by various sectors in various locations throughout Iran. The situation of Iran's ruling elite has been further aggravated by ferocious factional infighting, in turn worsened by the protests. Adding to that, international sanctions and major shifts in regional alignments due in large part to threats posed by Tehran to the security and stability of the region, have substantially weakened the entire ruling system.

Iranian society is simmering with deeply rooted rage. Iran is a powder keg, where anything, even a sudden rise in the price of fuel or eggs, could trigger a nationwide revolt. Khamenei and his regime are trying in vain to prevent the seismic shift they know is coming.

Successive Uprisings Since 2017, the Game Changer

The major uprisings across Iran since December 2017 clearly signal that the hoped-for revolution is within reach. Many, including Khamenei, see a regime-ending tsunami of protests and uprisings on the horizon. And the Iranian people see that change will not come by participating in the electoral farce; rather, participation would entrench the status quo with the veneer of legitimacy and permanence that an election bestows. The society seeks to overthrow the regime, not to vote for another corrupt murderous official of the theocratic establishment. The writing on the wall across Iran is: "My vote is for regime change."

The "*Dey* protests" of late December 2017 — January 2018, by all accounts and from different perspectives, marked an inflection point in the trajectory of both the protests and the political equations in Iran. The slogans targeted both Khamenei and Rouhani, the entire regime. The uprising did not call for elections or lost votes; it sought the ouster of the corrupt theocracy.

Protesters throw rocks at the security forces during a protest in August 2018 in Isfahan.

One slogan in particular, "Hard-liners, reformers, the game is now over," which started in Tehran and in a matter of hours was heard all over Iran, sent an unmistakable message: The Iranian people have no illusions about the possibility of reform or gradual change from within. They dispelled once and for all the fake, anti-Iranian narrative — still harbored by some policy circles — of "hardlines vs. moderates."

The November 2019 uprising encompassed nearly 200 cities and towns, and resulted in ever harsher repression by regime authorities. Whereas the earlier uprisings led to several dozen deaths from gunshots and torture, in 2019 the Islamic Revolutionary Guard Corps opened fire on the crowds almost immediately, killing approximately 1,500 people over the course of about two weeks. Later, Amnesty International issued a report detailing the systematic torture that protesters and activists were subjected to for months afterward.

These uprisings demonstrated that the Iranian people are now focused on overthrowing the regime, and no longer pin any hope on elections as a solution for attaining real, substantive change. Protesters targeted the

Several Basij thugs attack a protester with handguns and an ax during November 2019 uprising in city of Gorgan.

People carry the body of a protester shot by the IRGC forces in city of Shiraz during the November 2019 Uprising

regime's main symbols of repression, theft, and corruption. The people view the regime and all its factions as illegitimate. Indeed, the people have witnessed that at the height of every uprising, the "reformist" camp in effect joins ranks with its rival faction and provides political cover for the suppressive forces to quash the unrest.

The uprisings have evolved in focus, organization and objective, now clearly defined as overthrowing the corrupt theocratic regime. Their gains, especially those of the November 2019 strife, are irreversible. The faces of the 1,500 martyrs of that uprising, and the scenes of the many who were murdered in cold blood will persist in the Iranian psyche. They fuel the determination to reject the regime and its elections. As much as the murderous response to the protests and uprisings represents a risk to ordinary Iranian lives, it also serves to highlight the extent of the regime's anxiety and desperation; the mullahs feel genuinely threatened.

The anti-regime reverberations of the November uprising as well as the January 2020 shooting down of a Ukrainian airliner with 176 passengers,

"Down with Khamenei, down with the principle of Velayat-e faqih."

were major factors in the boycott of the 2020 parliamentary elections. Many of the regime's own officials and analysts view that boycott as a stunning setback to the theocracy, and speculate that a massive boycott in the 2021 presidential election would deal a lethal blow to the regime's political prowess and legitimacy.

The Economy & Corruption Weigh Heavily on Iran's Elections

Iran's clerical regime will hold its presidential elections on June 18. While Supreme Leader Ali Khamenei is pushing to have a large turnout as a display of his regime's legitimacy, Iranians are protesting daily with chants of "We will vote no more; we have not seen any justice," and "We will vote no more; we have heard enough lies."

There are several factors fueling their antipathy, including oppression, economic crises, systemic corruption, outrage over inept handling of the COVID-19 pandemic, and ultimately the Iranian people's desire for freedom and an end to the regime, so emphatically expressed during the nationwide uprisings since 2017, particularly in November 2019.

This brief intends to show how Iran's economic crises have pushed more people below the poverty line, and how the consequent financial and social misery is motivating them to boycott the upcoming presidential election. They see the corrupt ruling theocracy as their true enemy and the first and foremost cause of the economic crises. One of the most dominant slogans in the recent uprising has been, "Our enemy is right here; they lie when they say it is America."

How Did the Economy Reach This Point?

Since the mullahs seized power in Iran after the 1979 Revolution, the country has been on a path of negative growth and economic decline. Officials plundered the nation's wealth and resources, crushing industrial production and growth, all to further the regime's evil ends.

International sanctions were never the cause of Iran's economic ills, which is why their lifting following the nuclear deal in 2015 did not provide the cure. There are systemic, entrenched factors at play that

have to do with the nature and socio-political roots of the kleptocratic ruling system. The people are fed up, and despite the heavy repression, despite the threat of the coronavirus, and despite many other problems, they have taken to the streets to protest the injustice, corruption, and tyranny of their rulers.

Today, Iran's economy is controlled by what has become known as the "power and wealth mafia," a network of regime institutions and their affiliates who have made a fortune at the expense of the nation. Most of Iran's population lives in utter poverty, a situation that has only become worse during the COVID-19 outbreak and the regime's disregard for the pandemic's effect on the people's lives and the country's economy.

Hossain Raghfar, one of the regime's top economists, told the state-run *Ressalat* in October 2020 that "The problem of the national economy is not the U.S. or sanctions. The main economic problems are lies, deception, and blaming others in order to divert the public mind from the bitter realities that domestic politics have brought upon the people."

"Misery Index" Soaring

In recent years, Iran has been one of the top four countries in the world in terms of the "misery index," defined as "the sum of current, seasonally adjusted unemployment plus the current inflation rate. According to official data, the misery index reached 19.8 percent in 2017, jumped to 39 percent in 2018, and reached 45.5 percent in 2019. Estimates show that this index is at 70 percent this year," according to a Feb 16 report by the state run *Hamdeli* daily.

The increasingly miserable state of the economy reflects itself in the daily lives of the Iranian people. The destructive policies of the regime have caused an unbridled rise in the price of fruits and vegetables, many of which have become completely out of reach of a large part of the population. Other basic goods, including meat, rice and poultry, are also becoming more and more expensive.

"Next year's inflation rate will be 40% higher [than the previous year's]. This means absolute poverty," said Abbas Akhundi, former Minister of Urban Development, on April 6.

"An end to hunger is also our inalienable right."

60 Million Living Below the Poverty Line

To put this in perspective, the average income of a working family is 15 to 20 million rials. The poverty line, however, is 100 million rials, i.e. at least five times what workers earn. According to the regime's official statistics, more than 60 million of Iran's population of 80 million live below the poverty line.

"While according to the Central Bank, the country's per-capita income in 2019 decreased by nearly 33 percent in comparison to 2011, with the outbreak of COVID-19 in 2020, the country's economy faced a new shock," the Tasnim news agency reported on January 19, 2021.

Years ago, the poverty line was determined by the life index of people living in the lower third decile of society. But now, the poverty line sits on top of the middle class. "Over the last three

The nation's poor sort through garbage to make ends meet.

years, we have seen an exponential increase in the cost of living in Iran, which has pushed the poverty line to the middle of the seventh decile… We are seeing the middle class approaching the lower class, as many studies have shown that the poverty line in Tehran has reached 100 million rials," said university professor Zahra Karimi last November, according to Tasnim News Agency, affiliated with the IRGC.

Will a Return to the JCPOA Cure the Economy?

The state-run media acknowledge that, even if the regime manages to sell oil and natural resources in 2021, it still will not have a serious impact on people's lives, especially on the lives of the lower and poorer classes. On March 30, *Tejarat* daily reported, "The country's economic growth is forecast to be positive in 2021… but due to the lack of serious impact on employment, the people's living conditions are unlikely to change much."

Mohsen Rezaee, the head of the Expediency Council, said on March 6: "From 2013 [the beginning of Rouhani's presidency] until now, the people's buying power has decreased considerably. An important part of the problems is not due to sanctions, but to management issues. Negligence has resulted in the devaluation of the national currency relative to foreign currencies. And you can see the conditions of the stock market."

Systemic Corruption

Iran's regime has been plagued by institutionalized financial corruption since its inception. According to Transparency International, Iran ranks 149 among 180 countries on the corruption perceptions index.

On May 3, during the session of the Supreme Judiciary Council, Attorney General Ali Alghazi Mehr acknowledged another major embezzlement case in the 2016-2018 period, which involved $30.2 billion and 60 tons of gold. It has also been reported that a criminal case has been filed against Valiollah Seif, the former president of the Central Bank. Additionally, Gholamhossein Esmaili, the spokesperson of the Judiciary, confirmed the arrest of 200 Judiciary staffers on May 11.

These and many other cases demonstrate that corruption and embezzlement are deeply ingrained in the structure of this regime. The flipside of this mega-corruption is, of course, the tragic situation of the Iranian people, who have to find shelter in graves, food in garbage, and sell their body organs to sustain themselves. With the revelation of every one of these cases, the people become even more outraged and determined to overthrow this regime and bring decency back to their country.

Economic Issues, Corruption Sparked Recent Uprisings

All major uprisings since 2017 were triggered by economic issues and high prices. On December 28, 2017, the people of the northeastern city Mashhad, considered a bastion of the ruling regime, erupted in protest over the price of eggs and other basic food staples. They chanted, "Death

"If prices weren't so high the people wouldn't be here."

to high prices," "The 'moderate' government's promises are empty," and "One less embezzlement would solve our problem." The protests soon became political, with slogans such as "Death to the dictator, death to Rouhani," and in less than 48 hours had turned into a nationwide uprising. The 2018 Kazeroun revolt and Tehran bazaar unrest were all protests over economic issues and poverty.

The nationwide uprising that erupted on November 15, 2019 and spread to over 180 cities in all 31 provinces of Iran, was sparked by a gasoline price hike, by as much as 300 percent. The protests, however, rapidly expanded and changed focus, targeting the entire regime. Besides IRGC and Basij centers of suppression, over one thousand state-run banks were attacked by protesters who saw these financial institutions as symbols of the regime's corruption and plundering of their wealth and resources.

Empty Tables, Public Outrage, An Electoral Boycott

With over 50% of Iranians now having access to smartphones and a multitude of social media platforms, they see in real time that as vital items such as meat, dairy product, poultry, and eggs disappear from their tables, the tables of the ruling elite and their families become more colorful and richer by the day.

On May 5, Saeed Mohammad, the former commander of the Khatam-al Anbiya Construction Headquarters, the largest economic holding of the Guards and one of the candidates disqualified after nominating himself for the presidency, wrote in a letter to all candidates: "The people are tired and angry about the current situation, their empty tables, and the inefficiency and corruption of the rulers of the Islamic Republic, and want a great change in the style of governing."

Long lines for poultry as prices have been skyrocketing.

In the letter, Mohammad stressed that "The people are tired of the factionalism, hypocrisy, discrimination, and injustice of the political and economic aristocracy, of unkept promises, and of hearing the daily news of corruption cases."

It is worth noting that the Khatam Al-Anbiya Garrison is itself one of the major embodiments of economic corruption and plunder. So, while Mohammad's words are notable, the bigger takeaway is the fact that he, notorious for his corruption, had nominated himself for president. That says a great deal about the character of the candidates.

Of course, the people will ultimately respond to all this corruption and inefficiency in their own way, by boycotting the election, and casting their vote with protests and uprisings.

Historic Boycott Expected

The ruling theocracy faces three major obstacles in holding this year's presidential election: the potential for social protests, the reaction to Khamenei's consolidation of power by rival factions, and a low election turnout.

On May 20, the state-run website Andishe Moaser quoted Deputy Judiciary Chief Gholam-Hossein Mohseni-Eje'i as saying, "Under the current circumstances, the election is the country's most important event, and the enemies will increase their efforts to weaken us to reach their evil goals."

The Deputy commander of the State Security Forces, Qassem Rezai, has also warned that "The enemy wants our elections not to be passionate... Our responsibility is to maintain the security of the election, and we will prepare for those who try to disturb the peace."

The regime is deeply fearful, and knows full well that the situation in the streets is a powder keg, which makes the anticipated low turnout a nightmarish prospect that all factions are struggling to avoid. On May 11, the regime's Supreme Leader, Ali Khamenei, warned, "Primarily,

Protesters' chant in nationwide uprisings: "Hardliners, reformers, the game is now over"

a large popular turnout is important since [a low turnout] could turn into a security problem."

Other regime officials and media outlets are also sounding the alarm, using phrases like "cold and silent election atmosphere," and emphasizing "the people's disillusionment, especially the youth, with politics," with "repetitive and tested faces," with "institutional inefficiency" and with "fake politicians on both sides, reformists and hardliners."

Widespread Electoral Apathy

There are many factors for this apathy explicitly expressed by many segments of the society. The 2021 presidential election is impacted by a series of major social upheavals, including uprisings in 2017, 2018, and 2019, whose main slogans were: "Hardliners, reformers, the game is now over," "Death to the dictator," and "Our enemy is right here; they lie when say it is America." In addition, the economy has been ravaged by systemic state corruption and the disastrous handling of the COVID-19 pandemic.

The Iranian people have shown, at great cost to their lives, that they emphatically reject the regime and all its factions and seek its ouster. They see the phony "reformists vs hardliners" narrative as a ploy to give the regime a veneer of legitimacy and provide its apologists and advocates abroad with talking points. They know first-hand that under this regime and its constitution, elections are merely a farce and will not fundamentally change anything. The so-called hardliners and reformists ultimately work together to preserve the regime.

On May 16, Mohammad Ali Abtahi, Chief of Staff of former President Mohammad Khatami, acknowledged, "This time the main challenger in the election is neither a Reformist nor a Principlist; it is low voter turnout."

In recent weeks, many sectors of the society have declared their lack of interest in voting. "We have seen no justice and we will not vote!" is a common slogan heard these days in different protests reported from various cities across the country. From small investors in the stock market to pensioners, nurses, farmers, and workers, a large number of Iranian communities are deeply dissatisfied with the current economic situation and their living conditions. On May 1, workers took to the streets in more than 20 cities and declared their determination to boycott the elections with the slogans "We will not vote, we've heard too many lies" and "Every worker must boycott the elections."

The expected nationwide boycott is not a passive response to the ruling theocracy. It is indeed the flipside of the nationwide desire for regime change. Boycotts are pervasive in protests across Iran these days. People know that the only solution is to take to the streets. That message was conveyed in the most emphatic way in the streets of Iran during the November 2019 uprising, during which over 1,500 protesters were murdered in cold blood by the IRGC's thugs following Khamenei's shoot-to-kill order.

On May 16, 2021, retirees and pensioners as well as the teachers of the "literacy movement" staged protests in Tehran and 14 other cities against the dire economic situation, declaring, "We will vote no more; we have heard too many lies," and "We will not rest until we get our rights."

Earlier in May, several mothers of the martyrs of the November 2019 uprising bravely called for an election boycott with chants of "Our vote is regime change" and "Overthrow this regime."

Call for a Boycott by Maryam Rajavi

Following a call by the Iranian Resistance's President-elect, Maryam Rajavi, the MEK network in Iran has been leading a nationwide campaign to boycott Iran's sham presidential election. In various cities, graffiti by Resistance Units demands: "No to the sham elections," "My vote is for regime change," "Boycotting the election sham is a patriotic duty," "No to the mullahs' rule, no to religious tyranny, yes to a democratic republic," and "Down with Khamenei."

Maryam Rajavi
@Maryam_Rajavi

The Iranian people have said and will say NO to the mullahs' regime, NO to religious fascism, NO to despotism, tyranny and pillage. YES to freedom, YES to the universal suffrage, and YES to a democratic republic. #Iran #BoycottIranShamElections

The Resistance Units in various cities, especially in Tehran, have posted banners and placards, written graffiti and distributed leaflets to encourage a massive boycott. These efforts have received widespread support from the public. In April alone, MEK Resistance Units organized

The MEK's Resistance Units in various cities post banners and placards, write graffiti and distribute leaflets to encourage a massive boycott.

campaigns every day in more than 250 locations in 27 provinces across Iran, including Tehran, Shiraz, Isfahan, Mashhad, Kermanshah, Nishabur, Iranshahr, Birjan, Ilam, Chalus, Ghaemshahr, Hamadan, Arak, Saveh, Lahijan, Gorgan, Saqqez, Kahnuj, Behbahan, Meshkin Shahr,

Astane Ashrafiyeh, Sabzevar, Anzali, Chalus, Esfarayen, Zahedan, and Khorramabad.

Meanwhile, the regime has increased its repressive measures in anticipation of unrest during the upcoming election. Any display or act of support for the MEK is harshly punished. In February, the regime resorted to mass arrests of MEK supporters and their family members and issued heavy sentences to many, as part of a nationwide campaign to quash the Resistance Units.

In a series of interviews with Simaye Azadi, the satellite television channel affiliated with the Iranian Resistance, many members of the Resistance Units have explained their motivation for joining this nationwide movement. One member said, "I have a bachelor's degree, but I'm working as a construction worker. There are many people like me who are suffering from discrimination and pressure. The MEK is the only group that has paid the heavy price for freedom and commitment."

Another individual explained how she overcame her fear of arrest while placing a poster of Maryam Rajavi in Tehran. "Two people saw me while I was installing a banner of Maryam Rajavi, but I decided that I would risk my life for the freedom of my country," she said.

"These mullahs are sucking our blood; enough is enough, we must overthrow them. Their only fear is the MEK, and so the MEK is our only hope for change... Installing anti-regime posters in the streets under the threat of arrest is not an easy task, but this is our struggle against the mullahs," said another.

Rally by MEK supporters abroad calling for boycott of the election

The ongoing efforts of the MEK Resistance Units lay bare the enormous potential within Iranian society for change, and the faith in the MEK. In the last two and a half years, the MEK Resistance Units have played a major role in organizing and leading five nationwide protests.

Many regime officials have acknowledged their role. On November 17, 2019, Khamenei referred to the MEK as a "wicked and criminal collective" who are "constantly encouraging and inviting people on social networks and elsewhere to conduct these evil acts." A few days later, on November 24, Ali Shamkhani, Secretary for the Supreme National Security Council, said: "I believe 34 MEK members have been arrested so far. A vast network of individuals, operating not under the MEK's name, but pursuing their line and modus operandi were also identified."

The Regime's Worst Nightmare

The regime's studies of public attitudes have predicted and expressed grave concern over a lower turnout for the presidential election than the March 2020 parliamentary election farce. The Interior Ministry publicly put the March 2020 election turnout at 42% nationwide, and about 20% for Tehran. However, an internal Ministry report admitted the turnout was 20% nationwide and 9% in Tehran.

Officials and state-controlled media have expressed concern about a massive boycott, with Khamenei expressing his dread with his usual deflection to "foreign enemies."

On May 3, the daily *Javan*, affiliated with the IRGC, wrote, "The main polarization that the enemy has designed for the 2021 elections, is the decision to vote or not to vote."

"Political polarization will result in social gaps that heighten social radicalization," according to the *Vatan-e Emrouz* daily, backing the Principlist camp, on April 27.

Mostaghel, affiliated with the other camp, also sounded the alarm that the real winner of this factional "polarization" will be the Iranian Resistance. On May 10, it wrote: "Do they [the Principlist camp] know that their actions create wide rifts in the system that the enemy will use? ... Why don't the [members of the rival faction] see that the sworn enemy of the system, the MEK, who have no desire but the [regime's] overthrow, call for riots and protests daily? Don't they see that this old enemy has invested in creating rifts, even in the run-up to the presidential election?"

The daily *Arman Meli*, affiliated with the so-called Moderates/Reformist camp, wrote on May 5, "Encouraging people to participate in the election requires a miracle... There is no doubt that the Islamic Republic as a political system is facing a crisis due to its many internal and external dilemmas and its 40-year track record. This crisis has significant consequences in reducing the people's participation in the election... It seems that a miracle is needed for a serious turnout..."

Other admissions by state-run media of both factions underscoring the expected low turnout, include:

▸ **Donya-e Eqtesad — March 24, 2021**
Remarks by Khamenei: "The enemy doesn't want [the election to be an opportunity to show popular support for the regime]. As we draw close to the election, they start saying there is no freedom. Sometimes they say it has been engineered ... to make voters indifferent... They dishearten the people and say, your vote doesn't make a difference, won't improve the situation. They are full force behind these things, and they make maximum use of social media ..."

▸ **Shargh — April 21, 2021**
Mahmoud Sadeghi, a former member of the Majlis (Parliament): "The main challenge in the upcoming presidential election is the drop in public confidence, for various important reasons, about making a difference in the fate of the country."

▸ **Jahane Sanat — April 25, 2021**
"Citizens are cold regarding the election, and it seems that their ice cannot be melted... Iranians are so preoccupied with everyday life and resolving daily problems that they do not think at all about an election in which nothing will be determined."

▸ **Jahane Sanat — April 25, 2021**
"A large part of society is ignoring the ballot box due to public dissatisfaction, coronavirus mismanagement, bad economic conditions, low wages, as well as the official indifference to the events [uprisings] of January 2018 and November 2019. Given the current situation, it is unlikely that the turnout will be significant."

- **Mostaghel — May 8, 2021**

  "We will soon reach the 13th presidential election and unlike previous terms, we see no motivation or attention being paid by the public. Apparently, the Rouhani government's performance has in simple terms conveyed the incompetence, failure, and inefficiency of all Iranian governments to the voters."

- **Arman Meli — May 11, 2021**

  Sadegh Maleki, political analyst: "Never in the last four decades has the political climate in the run-up to the presidential election been so cold and indifferent. This is the result of a process, and the most important reasons for it are the structural inefficiency and the fake politicians posing as reformists and fundamentalists. People are tired of being toyed with, and their cold shoulder to the ballot box is not just a political act, but an important message to fundamentally change things."

- **Etemad daily — May 20, 2021**

  Seyed Mohammad Sadr, a member of the Expediency Council, said: "If participation in the election is sparse, it means that the Islamic Republic has lost its base. This will have international consequences. Today, the Islamic Republic has enemies in Israel, dissidents seeking its overthrow, and the United States, and they are all waiting for a problem in Iran's affairs to say that the Islamic Republic has lost its popular base and its collapse is near."

- **Jahan Sanat daily — May 18, 2021**

  "ISPA Polling Center published the results of its latest poll in May showing that only 11.4% of people follow presidential election news... Currently, according to social experts, there is a kind of public apathy and a political cold shoulder being shown to the election in the country. Of course, one of the reasons people have been turned off by the government and the political system is the slow vaccination process."

▶ **Sharq – May 18, 2021**
"A brief look at the statements and speeches of the candidates in the upcoming elections on June 18th represents the depth of phony politics, meaningless slogans, unachievable promises, and playing with people's fate and mocking their intelligence…

The Candidates

The regime initially lined up its usual lengthy list of candidates, all of whom are implicated in over four decades of terrorism, crimes against humanity, genocide, war crimes and plunder. The mass murderer and head of the regime's Judiciary, Ebrahim Raisi; the IRGC commander-turned Parliament Speaker, Ali Larijani; the First Vice President, Eshaq Jahangiri; and half a dozen IRGC commanders were among the top candidates.

Khamenei's Guardian Council only approved Ebrahim Raisi along with 6 others, most with little or no name recognition. Several candidates who had held key positions, including a former two-time president, Mahmoud Ahmadinejad; and a former vice-president, Eshaq Jahangiri, who was previously twice approved, were disqualified. However, the most significant purge was that of former three-time head of the legislative branch, and the Supreme Leader's ally, Ali Larijani, to pave the way for Khamenei's selected candidate, Raisi.

Ebrahim Raisi

Ebrahim Raisi stepped into Iran's political scene after the 1979 revolution as a pro-Khomeini cleric willing to carry out his mentor's every command. Born in 1960, Raisi started training as a cleric in Qom's seminary at 15, and entered the clerical regime's Judiciary from early on, as assistant prosecutor in Karaj (west of Tehran) when he was 19 years old. He became the prosecutor of the Revolutionary Court of Karaj when he was just 20, and rose to Judiciary Chief in 2019.

Ebrahim Raisi and Qassem Soleimani

Responsible for 1988 Massacre of Political Prisoners

In 1988, as Deputy Prosecutor of Tehran, Raisi was one of the four individuals appointed by Khomeini to carry out his infamous fatwa to massacre imprisoned activists of the People's Mojahedin Organization of Iran (PMOI/MEK). 30,000 political prisoners, primarily affiliated with the MEK, were summarily executed within a few months. An audiotape surfaced in summer 2016, after 28 years, of Khomeini's designated successor at the time, Hossein-Ali Montazeri, speaking with the "death committee" in Tehran, which included Raisi. Montazeri warned them that the executions would be considered as "the biggest crimes committed by the Islamic Republic."

In that meeting, about 20 days after the start of the killing spree, Montazeri questioned them about the execution of pregnant women and 15-year-old girls. It was subsequently exposed that Raisi was the most active and most ruthless member of the committee. True to form, after the public outcry over the 1988 Massacre, Raisi boasted on state TV, on June 2, 2020, "Well, these [MEK] should not be given a chance... These are the people to whom the Imam [Khomeini] said we shouldn't have shown any mercy, and the Imam knew them well."

Inflicting Violence on Dissidents

Raisi is currently the First Deputy Chairman of the Assembly of Experts. He was promoted to the position of Tehran Prosecutor in 1989 subsequent to Ali Khamenei's assuming the role of Supreme Leader. He held the position for five years, when he became Head of the Office of the Inspector General for a decade, from 1994 to 2004, and then Deputy Chief of the Judiciary for a decade, from 2004 to 2014. Khamenei appointed him as the Prosecutor General of the Special Court for the Clergy in 2014, a position he held until 2015.

Following the December 2009 uprising, Raisi is reported to have said: "*Moharebeh* (waging war against God) is sometimes by membership in an organization, like the *Monafeqin* (MEK). In the case of the organization of the *Monafeqin*, anyone who helps the organization of the *Monafeqin* in any way under any circumstances, because it is an organized movement, the title of *Moharebeh* applies." According to the Islamic Punishment Act, the punishment for *Moharebeh* is death.

Following the death of a senior cleric, Abbas Vaez-Tabasi, Khamenei appointed Raisi in 2016 as the Head of the Astan-e Quds Razavi foundation in Mashhad, northeast Iran, one of the regime's most important political and financial endowments controlling massive assets, land, buildings, and capital.

Khamenei appointed Raisi as Judiciary Chief in March 2019. Since then, he has directed the execution of 251 people in 2019, and 267 people in 2020, and scores of executions in 2021. Amnesty International reported that "The death penalty was increasingly used as a weapon of political repression against dissident protesters and members of ethnic minority groups" during Raisi's term. One particular case that drew international outcry was the brutal execution of Iranian sportsman and wrestler Navid Afkari.

He is expected to enter the race for president in the current cycle as a Principlist (pro-Khamenei faction).

Saeed Jalili

Saeed Jalili

Saeed Jalili is an Iranian regime official, who served as secretary of the Supreme National Security Council and also one of the regime's nuclear negotiators.

Born in the northeastern city of Mashhad on September 1, 1965, he served as a member of the paramilitary Bassij Force and the Islamic Revolutionary Guards Corps (IRGC) during the Iran-Iraq War of the 1980s. In 1989, Jalili began working at the regime's Foreign Ministry. In 2001, he was appointed into Supreme Leader Ali Khamenei's office as the senior director of policy planning.

During the presidency of Mahmoud Ahmadinejad, Jalili was appointed as a presidential advisor and as deputy foreign minister for European and American affairs, a position he held from 2005 to October 2007. In 2007, Jalili was appointed to oversee negotiations over the regime's nuclear program. He was also the secretary of the Supreme National Security Council until Ali Shamkhani took over the post in September 2013. Immediately after leaving office, Khamenei appointed him into the Expediency Council.

Jalili signed up for the presidential elections in 2013 but lost. He has also registered as a candidate in the 2021 presidential elections despite announcing earlier that he would not do so if Khamenei's preferred candidate, Ebrahim Raisi, would run.

Mohsen Rezaee

IRGC Major General Mohsen Rezaee

Mohsen Rezaee Mirgaha'ed, 67, a conservative politician, is an IRGC Major General best known for his appointment as IRGC Commander by Ruhollah Khomeini. He held the post from the IRGC's early years through the Iran-Iraq War and until 1997. He has run for Parliament once (lost in 2000), and for president three times (withdrew in 2005, lost in 2009, lost in 2013). He has been a member and secretary of the Expediency Discernment Council since 1997.

Rezaee is implicated in the 1994 bombing of the AMIA center in Buenos Aires, Argentina, that resulted in 85 deaths and hundreds of injuries. There is an outstanding Interpol warrant for his arrest on charges of "aggravated murder and damages."

Under Rezaee's 16-year tenure, the IRGC played an active role in repression at home, founding and sponsoring of foreign terrorist proxy groups throughout the region, including Hezbollah in Lebanon, and taking part in terrorist operations abroad, including the assassination of dissidents in Europe in Austria, Switzerland, Italy, Germany, and elsewhere.

On January 10, 2020, the US Department of Treasury placed Rezaee on its sanctions list for his role in "advancing the regime's destabilizing objectives."

His signature achievement in the Iran-Iraq War was the strategy of sending human waves of soldiers, in particular school children, as cannon fodder to clear the minefields, resulting in the deaths of hundreds of thousands of Iranians.

In November 2007, Interpol's General Assembly, its supreme governing body, voted in favor of publishing the Red Notices requested by the Argentinean National Central Bureau (NCB) for six individuals for their role in the 1994 bombing of AMIA building. Mohsen Rezaee, the IRGC Commander at the time of the bombing, was one of the six.

Mohsen Mehralizadeh

Mohsen Mehralizadeh

Mohsen Mehralizadeh was born 1956 in the city of Maragheh (Azerbaijan Province). In the early years after the 1979 Revolution, he helped in forming the paramilitary units in his hometown which would later become the Revolutionary Guards. In 1992, he became Vice President of Nuclear Plant Affairs of the Iranian Atomic Energy Organization. From 1997 to 2001, he was the Governor of Khorasan Province (Khamenei's home province).

In 2001, he joined Mohammad Khatami's government as a Vice President and head of the National Sports Organization. In 2005, the Guardian Council rejected his candidacy for the presidential election. The decision was reversed the next day when Khamenei personally intervened. He finished last among seven candidates. In 2017, he became Governor of Isfahan Province.

Alireza Zakani

Alireza Zakani

Alireza Zakani, born 1965 in Tehran, is a member of the pro-Khamenei United Front of the Principlists. At age 16, he served as a paramilitary member in the Irregular Warfare Headquarters while still attending high school. He rose to the rank of deputy intelligence commander in the 27th Mohammad Rassoul Allah Division. After the war, Zakani became the head of the student Basij organization, a volunteer paramilitary organization operating under the Iranian Revolutionary Guard.

In 2004, Zakani was elected to Parliament as a representative of Tehran. He ran for President in 2013 and 2017, but was disqualified by the Guardian Council both times. Zakani lost his Parliament seat in 2016, but returned in 2020. He is a staunch supporter of the Iranian role in the internal affairs of Iraq and Syria

Abdolnaser Hemmati

Abdolnaser Hemmati was born in 1957 in Hamedan Province. He started his affiliation with the Iranian regime during the Iran-Iraq War (1980—1988) as newsroom director for Islamic Republic of Iran Broadcasting (IRIB), where he was put in charge of war messaging. He continued with IRIB after the war as Director General until 1994. Later he worked in the banking and insurance sector. He was CEO of Bank Sina (2006—2013) and CEO of Bank Melli (2013—2018). Both banks were sanctioned by the Obama administration for servicing entities involved in Iran's nuclear and ballistic programs. Since 2018, he has been the Governor of the Iranian Central Bank.

Abdolnaser Hemmati

Amir-Hossein Ghazizadeh Hashemi

Amir-Hossein Ghazizadeh Hashemi

Amir Hossein Ghazizadeh Hashemi, born in 1971 in the northeastern city of Fariman, is a hardline politician of the pro-Khamenei Principlist faction. He has been a member of the regime's parliament for Mashhad and the Kalat electoral district in Razavi Khorasan Province since 2008. He was member of the Front of Islamic Revolution Stability (Principlist faction), and served as the party's spokesperson. In 2016, Hashemi was chosen as first deputy speaker in Parliament under Speaker Ali Larijiani. As deputy speaker, Hashemi expressed staunch support for Hamas and the Palestinian Islamic Jihad. In September 2020, he denounced the Abraham Accord as "apostasy."

The Selection Process

The Five Qualifications

Article 115 of the Constitution of the Islamic Republic of Iran states: "The President of the Republic must be elected from among the religious and political men who meet the following qualifications: Iranian origin, Iranian nationality, administrative leadership, clear past record, honesty and piety, believing in the fundamentals of the Islamic Republic of Iran and the official religion of the country."

The determination for whether a candidate meets these five qualifications falls on the Guardian Council. Article 91 of the Constitution mandates the creation of the "Guardian Council" (*shoray-e negahban*), which is comprised of six clerics handpicked by the Supreme Leader (*vali-e faqih*) and six jurists appointed by the head of the Judiciary (who himself is also appointed by the Supreme Leader), and approved by the Supreme Leader.

During the past 11 presidential elections, the Guardian Council has never vetted the candidates in accordance with Article 115. For example:

- ▶ Mahmoud Ahmadinejad, whose candidacy was approved twice previously and served as president for two terms, was rejected without explanation in 2017 and 2021.

- ▶ During the 2013 presidential elections, the candidacy of even Ali Akbar Hashemi Rafsanjani, who helped the regime appoint Ali Khamenei as the current Supreme Leader, and served two terms as president, was rejected by the Guardian Council.

Added Criteria to Restrict Registration

On May 5, 2021, the Guardian Council issued a directive outlining its new criteria for candidates contending in the 2021 presidential election. According to this directive, the candidates should be between 40 to 75 years old, they should hold at least a master's degree and have served in an executive position for at least four years. They should also possess a background as a former cabinet minister, or a governor-general, or mayor in a city with over two million population. Candidates should present clearance from police at the time of their registration. Military candidates should be major generals or higher in rank.

Proportion of rejected candidates in 13 presidential elections

The table below lists presidential candidates as well as the number of those approved by the Guardian Council:

Official statistics claimed by the Iranian regime in the past presidential elections						
Round	Date of Elections	Registered Candidates	Approved Candidates	% Approved	Voter Participation	Name of President
1	January 25, 1980	124	123	99.0%	67.0%	Abolhassan Banisadr
2	June 24, 1981	71	4	5.7%	64.0%	Mohammad-Ali Rajai
3	October 2, 1981	46	4	8.7%	64.0%	Seyyed Ali Khamenei
4	August 6, 1985	50	3	6.0%	55.0%	Seyyed Ali Khamenei
5	June 28, 1989	79	2	3.3%	55.0%	Ali-Akbar Hashemi Rafsanjani
6	June 11, 1993	128	4	3.1%	51.0%	Ali-Akbar Hashemi Rafsanjani
7	May 23, 1997	238	4	1.6%	80.0%	Mohammad Khatami
8	June 8, 2001	817	10	1.2%	67.0%	Mohammad Khatami
9	June 17, 2005	1014	8	0.8%	60.0%	Mahmoud Ahmadinejad
10	June 12, 2009	475	4	0.8%	85.0%	Mahmoud Ahmadinejad
11	June 14, 2013	686	8	1.2%	72.7%	Hassan Rouhani
12	May 19, 2017	1636	6	0.4%	73.3%	Hassan Rouhani
13	June 18, 2021	592	7	1.2%	??	??

The Guardian Council was not yet created during the first round of presidential elections in the clerical regime, which was established after the 1979 Revolution. At the time, former Supreme Leader Khomeini initially announced that anyone could become a presidential candidate and the people could choose their preferred option. However, after Massoud Rajavi, who enjoyed widespread popularity among various sectors of society, declared his candidacy, Khomeini changed his stance and declared that those who had not voted in favor of the Constitution could not become president. The organization then led by Rajavi, the People's Mojahedin Organization of Iran (PMOI/MEK), had boycotted the vote on the Constitution, rejecting its inclusion of the principle of *velayat-e faqih* (absolute rule of the clerics). Still, in announcing his candidacy, Massoud Rajavi had officially declared his willingness to comply with the Constitution.

Supreme Leader's 4 Filters for a President

In the *velayat-e faqih* system, the selection of a president is controlled and vetted by the Supreme Leader at four stages or points, to ensure that the president aligns with his wishes and mandates.

1. Personal approval: It is an unwritten rule that all candidates who end up being approved by the Guardian Council must have received permission from the Supreme Leader to run for president. Without exception, any candidate who has not received Khamenei's permission has not been approved. In addition to Ali Larijani in 2021, two other specific examples are Rafsanjani's candidacy in 2013 and Ahmadinejad's in 2017 and 2021:

a. As he described in his memoirs, Rafsanjani said that he was awaiting Khamenei's response to his candidacy until the last minutes of the deadline for registration. Khamenei refused to respond to Rafsanjani despite repeated phone calls to Khamenei's office. When Rafsanjani finally declared his candidacy in the final stretch of registration, observers were stunned to hear that the Guardian Council, at Khamenei's direction, had rejected Rafsanjani's candidacy.
b. In September 2016, Ahmadinejad met with Khamenei to request permission to run for president. However, Khamenei suggested that he should not declare his candidacy. Khamenei later announced publicly that he had recommended that Ahmadinejad not run in the next presidential elections. But when Ahmadinejad announced his candidacy in contradiction to Khamenei's directive, the Guardian Council rejected him without explanation.

2. Vetting of candidates by the Guardian Council: The Guardian Council selects a final list of presidential candidates in accordance with Article 115 of the Constitution. In 11 of the last 12 presidential elections, the percentage of approved candidates has been in the single digits (only once, ten candidates were approved). In recent years, that number has been reduced to less than one percent. The Guardian Council completes this process not on the basis of Article 115, but based on the explicit direction of the Supreme Leader. In a word, in every round, candidates are approved on the basis of Khamenei's determination of his regime's interests in that particular context.

3. Election-engineering: Among the candidates selected by Khamenei, and announced by the Guardian Council in every round, Khamenei and his faction have a stronger tendency towards some and therefore resort to organized rigging implemented by

security-intelligence organizations (the Islamic Revolutionary Guard Corps, Basij, plain clothes agents, etc.) to manipulate results. For example, in 2005, when Rafsanjani announced his candidacy at a time when Khamenei did not support it, according to a self-described multi-year engineering plan, enacted by the IRGC and coordinated by Brig. Gen. Baqir Zolqadr, Ahmadinejad was declared the winner.

4. Consent: Article 110 of the Constitution of the regime proffers extensive authority to the Supreme Leader. For example, paragraph 9 of Article 110 of the Constitution declares that the Supreme Leader must approve the election of the president. Unless and until he approves the election, the president has no authority to head the executive branch. Therefore, the approval is not a symbolic function. The president's legitimacy derives from the Supreme Leader's final approval after the election. The approval has a supervisory mechanism until the end of the president's term. If and when the president deviates from the determined principles (opposing the *velayat-e faqih*), his legitimacy and credibility will be revoked. On this basis, the final dismissal of the president is ordered by the Supreme Leader (a logical extension of the initial approval), after the vote of non-confidence by the parliament or a judicial ruling by the Judiciary. It was on this basis that Khomeini ordered the dismissal of the regime's first president, Banisadr.

Therefore, on the basis of these four filters, the president is in practical terms an appointee of the Supreme Leader and not an official elected by the populace. Even without regard to the engineered aspect of the elections and systematic vote rigging, the opinion and choice of the voters is essentially limited to the candidates selected by the Supreme Leader, and the "winner's" presidency is contingent on the continued approval of the Supreme Leader, who has full authority to retain or dismiss him.

In a speech on March 21, 2021, Khamenei set several criteria for his ideal president:

- "First of all, he must be competent...

- "Secondly, he must have faith. One cannot trust the faithless. A faithless person will sell off the country, the interests of the country, the people, and so he must be faithful... He must have both revolutionary and jihadi credentials and track record. He cannot work in a gentlemanly manner for a country with all these fundamental problems. A jihadi and revolutionary approach is necessary, and that is how he must act...

- "Try to find such characteristics in a presidential candidate.

- "Regarding the elections, the last point is that our dear nation should make the elections a symbol of national unity, and not a symbol of divisions and schisms. Not a symbol of two poles. Put aside these mistaken classifications of left and right..."

What's Ahead?

Clearly, Khamenei has decided that to protect his regime, he must do his utmost to ensure the victory of his chosen candidate, Ebrahim Raisi. Thus, his Guardian Council disqualified several longtime establishment figures, most significantly Ali Larijani, the former speaker of the regime's parliament, a senior advisor to Khamenei and a member of his inner circle.

Notorious for his key role, as a member of the "death committee," Raisi has been involved in the mass execution of as many as 30,000 political prisoners, primarily activists of the People's Mojahedin Organization of Iran (MEK), in summer 1988, and ordered hundreds of other executions in the early 1980s.

Battered by a series of uprisings since 2017, endemic corruption, a bankrupt economy, and particularly the crushing blow of the boycott of the 2020 parliamentary elections and the growing prowess of nationwide organized opposition, Khamenei finds himself increasingly weak and vulnerable. He has opted to close ranks and consolidate power in the hands of those absolutely loyal to him to prevent the seismic shift he knows is coming.

As such, Khamenei will rely heavily on Raisi as well as the IRGC to counter internal dissent, just as he will rely on the Quds Force to expand his proxies in Syria, Lebanon, Iraq and elsewhere in the region. It is no coincidence that a week before the Guardian Council's announcement of its approved candidates, the Supreme Leader's website published the congratulatory messages (and Khamenei's replies to them) from Islamic Jihad and Hamas leaders, praising the regime for helping the Islamic Jihad with advanced rockets and missiles in Gaza. The more isolated Khamenei finds himself at home, the more he needs to rely on his proxies abroad.

Bottom line, the 13th presidential election has already put the regime in a weaker situation, while putting an end to all the games and masquerades. Khamenei has overtly recognized that the true fight is between the people and the organized opposition who want freedom and democracy on the one side, and the entirety of his regime, including its soon to be "elected" president Ebrahim Raisi, on the other.

The international community should take note of the new realities of Iran, and look at the regime through a new prism. A weaker and more desperate regime is prone to far more concessions than before. Nevertheless, an unstable regime will not be a reliable or lasting partner.

The United States, Europe, and the countries in the region should look instead to the people of Iran and see them as the true partners, who do not seek money, or boots on the ground, and expect no one to do the fighting for them. Instead, they seek respect for their desire for freedom, and demand recognition of their right to determine their future and change their repressive regime. They also seek accountability for their repressive rulers, instead of concessions and economic benefits which only prolong their rule.

The U.S. Congress has spoken. The bi-partisan House Resolution 118, with over 235 co-sponsors in the 117th Congress, says it all, and the Administration should heed their call. The House Majority "stands with the people of Iran who are continuing to hold legitimate and peaceful protests against an oppressive and corrupt regime, and recognizes the rights of the Iranian people and their struggle to establish a democratic, secular, and nonnuclear Republic of Iran."

List of publications

List of Publications by the National Council of Resistance of Iran, U.S. Representative Office

IRAN - The Imperative to Reimpose UN Sanctions
August 2020, 108 pages

This report shows how the Iranian regime is involved in procuring and manufacturing weapons and military equipment with the objective of exporting terrorism and warmongering, regional meddling by sending weapons and missiles to expand terrorist attacks, and resorts to terrorism.

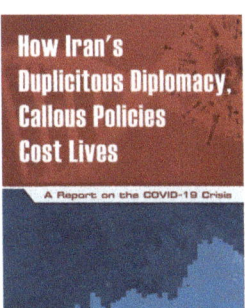

How Iran's Duplicitous Diplomacy, Callous Policies Cost Lives
A Report on the COVID-19 Crisis

April 2020, 84 pages

This report seeks to show that the Iranian Foreign Ministry's campaign to lift sanctions is replete with lies and misleading claims, with the goal of cynically exploiting the coronavirus pandemic to the regime's benefit In effect, the mullahs are causing the death of thousands of Iranians to preserve their own rule.

Iran's Emissaries of Terror

June 2019, 208 pages

This book explains the extent to which Tehran's embassies and diplomats are at the core of both the planning and execution of international terrorism targeting Iranian dissidents, as well as central to Tehran's direct and proxy terrorism against other countries.

Iran Doubles Down on Terror and Turmoil

November 2018, 63 pages

This book examines the regime's political and economic strategy, which revolves around terrorism and physical annihilation of opponents. Failing to quell growing popular protests, Tehran has bolstered domestic suppression with blatant terrorism and intimidation.

Iran Will Be Free: Speech by Maryam Rajavi

September 2018, 54 pages

Text of a keynote speech delivered by Mrs. Maryam Rajavi on June 30, 2018, at the Iranian Resistance's grand gathering in Paris, France explaining the path to freedom in Iran and what she envisions for future Iran.

Iran's Ballistic Buildup:
The March Toward Nuclear-Capable Missiles

May 2018, 136 pages

This manuscript surveys Iran's missile capabilities, including the underlying organization, structure, production, and development infrastructure, as well as launch facilities and the command centers. The book exposes the nexus between the regime's missile activities and its nuclear weapons program, including ties with North Korea.

Iran: Cyber Repression: How the IRGC Uses Cyberwarfare to Preserve the Theocracy

February 2018, 70 pages

This manuscript demonstrates how the Iranian regime, under the supervision and guidance of the IRGC and the Ministry of Intelligence and Security (MOIS), have employed new cyberwarfare and tactics in a desperate attempt to counter the growing dissent inside the country.

Iran: Where Mass Murderers Rule: The 1988 Massacre of 30,000 Political Prisoners and the Continuing Atrocities

November 2017, 161 pages

Iran: Where Mass Murderers Rule is an expose of the current rulers of Iran and their track record in human rights violations. The book details how 30,000 political prisoners fell victim to politicide during the summer of 1988 and showcases the egregious political extinction of a group of people.

Iran's Nuclear Core: Uninspected Military Sites, Vital to the Nuclear Weapons Program

October 2017, 52 pages

This book details how the nuclear weapons program is at the heart of, and not parallel to, the civil nuclear program of Iran. The program has been run by the Islamic Revolutionary Guards Corp (IRGC) since the beginning, and the main nuclear sites and nuclear research facilities have been hidden from the eyes of the United Nations nuclear watchdog.

Terrorist Training Camps in Iran: How Islamic Revolutionary Guards Corps Trains Foreign Fighters to Export Terrorism

June 2017, 56 pages

The book details how Islamic Revolutionary Guards Corps trains foreign fighters in 15 various camps in Iran to export terrorism. The IRGC has created a large directorate within its extraterritorial arm, the Quds Force, in order to expand its training of foreign mercenaries as part of the strategy to step up its meddling abroad in Syria, Iraq, Yemen, Bahrain, Afghanistan and elsewhere.

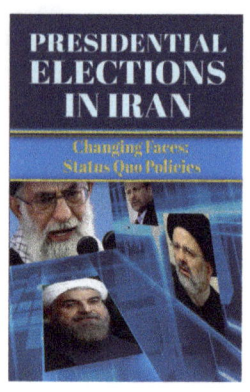

Presidential Elections in Iran: Changing Faces; Status Quo Policies

May 2017, 78 pages

The book reviews the past 11 presidential elections, demonstrating that the only criterion for qualifying as a candidate is practical and heartfelt allegiance to the Supreme Leader. An unelected vetting watchdog, the Guardian Council makes that determination.

The Rise of Iran's Revolutionary Guards' Financial Empire: How the Supreme Leader and the IRGC Rob the People to Fund International Terror

March 2017, 174 pages

This study shows how ownership of property in various spheres of the economy is gradually shifted from the population writ large towards a minority ruling elite comprised of the Supreme Leader's office and the IRGC, using 14 powerhouses, and how the money ends up funding terrorism worldwide.

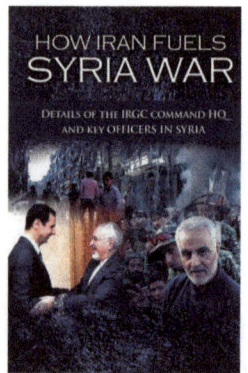

How Iran Fuels Syria War: Details of the IRGC Command HQ and Key Officers in Syria

November 2016, 74 pages

This book examines how the Iranian regime has effectively engaged in the military occupation of Syria by marshaling 70,000 forces, including the Islamic Revolutionary Guard Corps (IRGC) and mercenaries from other countries into Syria; is paying monthly salaries to over 250,000 militias and agents to prolong the conflict; and divided the country into 5 zones of conflict, establishing 18 command, logistics and operations centers.

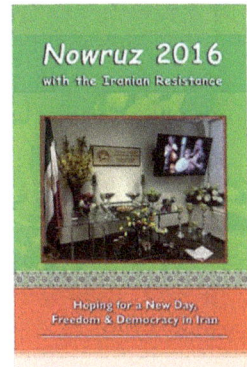

Nowruz 2016 with the Iranian Resistance: Hoping for a New Day, Freedom and Democracy in Iran

April 2016, 36 pages

This book describes Iranian New Year, Nowruz celebrations at the Washington office of Iran's parliament-in-exile, the National Council of Resistance of Iran. The yearly event marks the beginning of spring. It includes select speeches by dignitaries who have attended the NCRIUS Nowruz celebrations.

The 2016 Vote in Iran's Theocracy: An analysis of Parliamentary & Assembly of Experts Elections

February 2016, 70 pages

This book examines all the relevant data about the 2016 Assembly of Experts as well as Parliamentary elections ahead of the February 2016 elections. It looks at the history of elections since the revolution in 1979 and highlights the current intensified infighting among the various factions of the Iranian regime.

IRAN: A Writ of Deception and Cover-up: Iranian Regime's Secret Committee Hid Military Dimensions of its Nuclear Program

February 2016, 30 pages

The book provides details about a top-secret committee in charge of forging response to the International Atomic Energy Agency (IAEA) regarding the Possible Military Dimensions (PMD) of Tehran's nuclear program, including those related to the detonators called EBW (Exploding Bridge Wire), an integral part of developing an implosion type nuclear device.

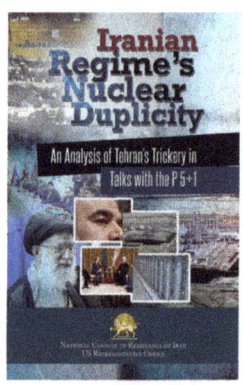

Iranian Regime's Nuclear Duplicity: An Analysis of Tehran's Trickery in Talks with the P 5+1

January 2016, 74 pages

This book examines Iran's behavior throughout the negotiations process in an effort to inform the current dialogue on a potential agreement. Drawing on both publicly available sources and those within Iran, the book focuses on two major periods of intense negotiations with the regime: 2003-2004 and 2013-2015.

Key to Countering Islamic Fundamentalism: Maryam Rajavi? Testimony To The U.S. House Foreign Affairs Committee

June 2015, 68 pages

Testimony before U.S. House Foreign Affairs Committee's subcommittee on Terrorism, non-Proliferation, and Trade discussing ISIS and Islamic fundamentalism. The book contains Maryam Rajavi's full testimony as well as the question and answer by representatives.

Meet the National Council of Resistance of Iran

June 2014, 150 pages

Meet the National Council of Resistance of Iran discusses what NCRI stands for, what its platform is, and why a vision for a free, democratic, secular, non-nuclear republic in Iran would serve world peace.

How Iran Regime Cheated the World: Tehran's Systematic Efforts to Cover Up its Nuclear Weapons Program

June 2014, 50 pages

The monograph discusses the Iranian regime's report card as far as it relates to being transparent when addressing the international community's concerns about the true nature and the ultimate purpose of its nuclear program.

About NCRI-US

National Council of Resistance of Iran-US Representative Office acts as the Washington office for Iran's Parliament-in-exile, which is dedicated to the establishment of a democratic, secular, non-nuclear republic in Iran.

NCRI-US, registered as a non-profit tax-exempt organization, has been instrumental in exposing many nuclear sites of Iran, including the sites in Natanz, and Arak, the biological and chemical weapons program of Iran, as well as its ambitious ballistic missile program.

NCRI-US has also exposed the terrorist network of the Iranian regime, including its involvement in the bombing of Khobar Towers in Saudi Arabia, the Jewish Community Center in Argentina, its fueling of sectarian violence in Iraq and Syria, and its malign activities in other parts of the Middle East.

Visit our website at www.ncrius.org

You may follow us on   twitter   @ncrius

Follow us on   facebook   NCRIUS

You can also find us on   Instagram   NCRIUS

www.ingramcontent.com/pod-product-compliance
Lightning Source LLC
Chambersburg PA
CBHW051359110526
44592CB00023B/2888